FOSSILS
~ AND ~
BONES

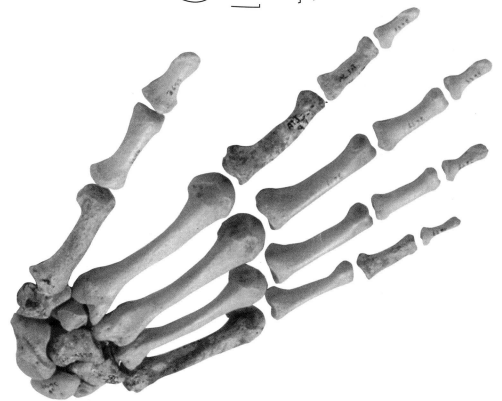

Saviour Pirotta

RSVP

RAINTREE
STECK-VAUGHN
P U B L I S H E R S
The Steck-Vaughn Company

Austin, Texas

THE
REMARKABLE
WORLD

Published by Raintree Steck-Vaughn Publishers, an imprint of Steck-Vaughn Company

Library of Congress Cataloging-in-Publication Data
Pirotta, Saviour.
Fossils and bones / Saviour Pirotta.
    p.   cm.—(Remarkable world)
Includes bibliographical references and index.
Summary: Describes how fossils are formed, different kinds that have been discovered, and what has been learned from them.
ISBN 0-8172-4542-1
1. Fossils—Juvenile literature.
[1. Fossils.]
I. Title. II. Series: Remarkable world (Austin, Tex.)
QE714.5.P57   1997
560—dc20   96-31734

Printed in Italy. Bound in the United States.
1 2 3 4 5 6 7 8 9 0 01 00 99 98 97

Picture acknowledgments
Bruce Coleman Ltd. 19b/Jane Burton, 40b/J Cancalosi, 42t/Kim Taylor; C.M. Dixon *front cover* center left, 9b, 14t, 20, 22t, 26t, 37b; Frank Lane Picture Agency 13b/D. Hosking; Hulton Deutsch 6t, 24t, 37c, 41t, 43t, 44b; Image Select 6b, 32t; Mary Evans Picture Library 11b, 41b; John Massey Stewart 25t; Museo Civico Di Storia Naturale di Verona, Italy 22b; Natural History Museum, London *front cover* main pic, 12b, 15b, 16b, 17b, 18t, 19t, 23, 24b, 26–27, 29b, 30 both, 33t/A Sutcliffe, 33b, 35t, 44t; Novosti (London) 36b, 38b, 39; Photri *front cover* bottom left; Planet Earth Pictures 45b/P. Scoones; Science Photo Library 4t/Peter Menzel, 4b/John Reader, 10t/John Reader, 11t/Peter Menzel, 12c/Sinclair Stammers, 17t/Sinclair Stammers, 21t/Claude Nuridsany and Marie Perennou, 25b/Peter Menzel, 29t/Sheila Terry, 31/John Reader, 31b, 34t/John Reader, 34b/John Reader, 37t/Alexander Tsiaras; Tony Stone Images 8b/Howard Grey, 15t/Nick Vedros, 43b/Art Wolfe; Roger Viollet 13c; Michael Voorhies 7b, 8t; Dave Wicks 28 both; Zefa 12t. The artwork is by Peter Bull.

CONTENTS

WHAT BONES AND FOSSILS TELL US

PEOPLE have been studying the remains of dead plants, animals, fish, and people since the fifth century B.C. During the last 300 years, these remains have helped us to get a clear picture of human history as well as that of our planet.

Sir Richard Owen, surrounded by fossil dinosaur bones

Two palaeontologists reconstruct the fossil skeleton of a plesiosaur—a meat-eating dinosaur that lived in water. The remains are about 120 million years old.

As dead as a *Dinornis*

Sir Richard Owen was a famous Victorian zoologist and palaeontologist. In 1839, a sailor who had just returned home from New Zealand gave Owen a 6-inch-long bone. Sir Richard guessed that it belonged to a type of bird that no longer existed, which would have been about 10 feet tall. He called it *Dinornis,* or the moa.

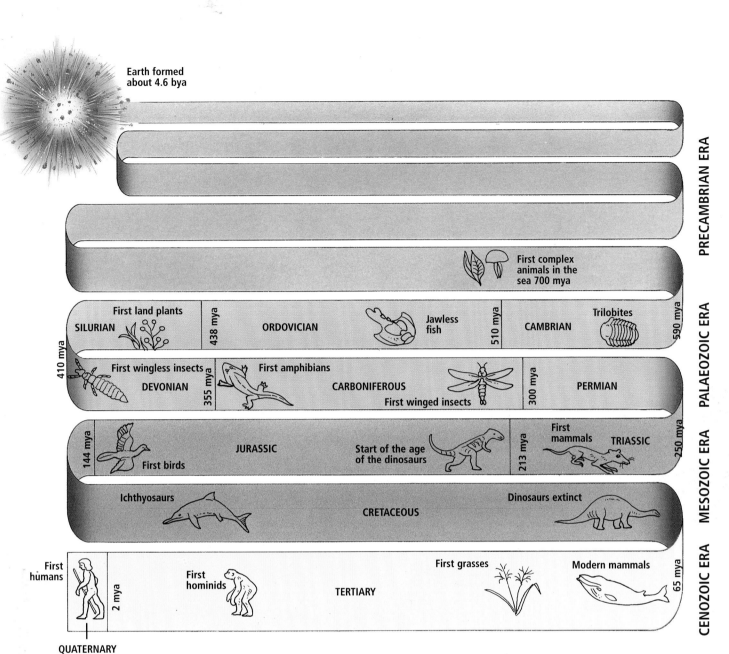

Earth formed about 4.6 bya

PRECAMBRIAN ERA

First complex animals in the sea 700 mya

PALAEOZOIC ERA

First land plants
SILURIAN
438 mya
ORDOVICIAN
Jawless fish
510 mya
CAMBRIAN
Trilobites
590 mya

410 mya

First wingless insects
DEVONIAN
355 mya
First amphibians
CARBONIFEROUS
First winged insects
300 mya
PERMIAN

MESOZOIC ERA

144 mya
JURASSIC
First birds
Start of the age of the dinosaurs
213 mya
First mammals
TRIASSIC
250 mya

Ichthyosaurs
CRETACEOUS
Dinosaurs extinct

CENOZOIC ERA

First humans
2 mya
First hominids
TERTIARY
First grasses
Modern mammals
65 mya

QUATERNARY

Other scientists were very doubtful, but Owen was right. Ten years later, he had collected enough bones to build a whole moa skeleton. He had also been correct about the moa being flightless—it had no wings.

In 1936, a horse belonging to Joseph Hogden died while carrying a heavy load of wood in Pyramid Valley, New Zealand. Joseph and his son Rob decided to bury the horse right there.

The time since Earth formed is divided into eras. These are then broken down into periods, such as the Jurassic. (mya = million years ago; bya = billion years ago)

A moa skeleton shown next to a human to give an idea of its size. The moa died out between 700 and 500 years ago.

A map of New Zealand showing the location of Pyramid Valley

They got shovels and started to dig an enormous hole in a swamp.

"This place is full of bones already," said Rob.

Joseph looked at the bones that his shovel had turned up. They were unlike any he had seen before. He reported the find and soon the swamp was swarming with palaeontologists (scientists who study fossils). In the first year, they dug up fifty bird skeletons, but not one of them was complete: They all had their skulls missing. The poor birds had mistakenly stepped into the mud and had been sucked under. As they fought for their last breath, giant eagles had attacked them and pulled off their heads.

About 2,400 bird skeletons were found in the swamps of Pyramid Valley. Many of them belonged to the giant moas. Some had been sucked quickly into the mud—they still had their heads attached to their necks.

More moa bones were discovered in ancient Maori settlements. This showed that they were still alive when the Maoris first went to New Zealand, about 1,200 years ago. European settlers also

How the moa might have looked when it was alive. It was related to the kiwi—some of them can be seen around the moa's feet.

Dead creature's flesh eaten by scavenging animals and bacteria

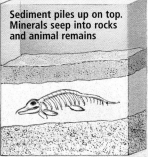

Sediment piles up on top. Minerals seep into rocks and animal remains

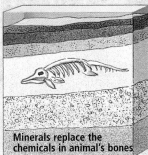

Minerals replace the chemicals in animal's bones

Rocks lifted up and become dry land. Fossil exposed

Fossils are formed over millions of years. This illustration shows how a dead animal becomes a fossil and leaves its imprint forever.

What is a fossil?

Fossils are the preserved remains of living organisms. When an organism dies, its body usually rots away. However, plants, animals, and occasionally people may become trapped in a substance that prevents their decay. This could be anything from sand, mud, and peat to tar and ice. Over millions of years, the trapped organism is chemically altered and turns to rock. Often only the hard part, like the shell or the backbone, survives to become fossilized. Sometimes, the dead creature disappears completely, leaving only its shape imprinted or cast in the stone.

One of the oldest known fossils is a bacterium from rocks known as the Fig Tree Formation in South Africa that is believed to be 3.4 billion years old.

reported seeing smaller species of the bird in the nineteenth century. However, the last moas disappeared soon after.

A lake full of bones
Ten million years ago, a crowd of animals went to drink at a watering hole in what is now Nebraska. As the thirsty creatures drank, a huge cloud of volcanic ash drifted across the Great Plains. Blinded and confused, the animals panicked and tried to escape, but they were all trapped. Within days, every single animal was dead. The ash kept falling until all their corpses were buried.

These fossil skeletons of rhinos were discovered in Nebraska in 1978. They are about ten million years old.

In 1978 an American palaeontologist, Michael Voorhies, discovered the site of the watering hole. He found two hundred fossilized skeletons, including a herd of rhinoceroses with their babies, as well as camels, turtles, three-toed horses, birds, saber-toothed cats, and a crane. One of the rhinos was carrying an unborn calf that also fossilized. Many of the skeletons were the most complete examples of their kind that have ever been found.

One of Michael Voorhies's palaeontologists carefully uncovers a fossilized skeleton.

Trapped in amber

A prehistoric mosquito sat on the back of a dinosaur, sucking the animal's blood. The dinosaur moved and the insect, startled, flew away. Feeling full and drowsy, it settled for a rest on a tree. It never got up again, because resin dripped out of the tree trunk and trapped the insect. Over millions of years, the resin turned into amber and the prehistoric mosquito was perfectly preserved.

Prehistoric insects trapped in amber. Insects were the first creatures to take to the sky.

Insects

The earliest insect fossils date from the Devonian period, which lasted from 410 million years ago to 355 million years ago. They are examples of collembolas, or springtails—wingless creatures that moved by jumping.

The first winged insects, called *pterygotes*, appeared during the Carboniferous period, 355 to 300 million years ago. At first, the insects had flat plates running down their bodies. Over time, they started to flap the plates, which gradually developed into wings. These early wings were usually veined and almost transparent, like the wings of modern damselflies.

There are now at least two million known types of insects. Experts think there might be as many as twelve million more waiting to be discovered.

Early dragonflies were huge, with a wingspan of nearly 20 inches. This dragonfly fossil is from the Jurassic period.

UNDERSTANDING THE FIRST FOSSILS

A plate of fossil "dragons" teeth and a Chinese medicine recipe

UNTIL the middle of the seventeenth century, most people had no idea what fossils really were. They mistook them for all kinds of strange, unlikely things—frozen thunderbolts, congealed snake spit, and even the devil's toenails. Some people believed that fossils grew out of the soil and lay waiting to be picked, much like flowers. Sometimes ancient people were buried with fossils as good luck charms or to ward off evil spirits.

The Chinese used prehistoric fossils for medicine, believing them to be the bones of dead dragons. They ground them up and ate them to cure all kinds of illnesses. About a hundred years ago, a German named Herr Heberer bought many fossils from Chinese medicine shops.

He took them to Europe, where experts studied them and discovered that they belonged to extinct bears, giraffes, and rhinoceroses. Even today, many Chinese people believe that ground lampshells can cure upset stomachs and cataracts in the eyes.

The fossilized teeth of the *Lepidotes,* a 6-foot-long fish, were also believed to have useful medicinal properties. In the Middle Ages in Europe, people took them to prevent food poisoning or to cure epilepsy. They had no idea that the round, brown stones were the teeth of extinct fish. They thought they were toadstones—little pebbles that were believed to grow inside the heads of toads.

The well-preserved fossil remains of a prehistoric fish called *Lepidotes.* Its scales and bony head can be seen clearly. This fossil is about 30 inches long and was found in Germany.

Not just a pile of old rocks

The first person to realize that fossils were the remains of dead creatures was probably the Renaissance artist Leonardo da Vinci (1452–1519). He noticed that fossilized shells looked just like the shells he saw in the Mediterranean Sea. People liked this idea, and said that the shells must have been swept there by the great flood described in the Old Testament of the Bible.

Leonardo laughed at them. He believed, correctly, that the rocks the fossils had been found in were once part of the seabed. He suggested that studying fossils would help to unlock the history of the world's ancient past, but no one would listen. Palaeontology—the scientific study of fossils—was not taken seriously until the middle of the seventeenth century.

A Danish doctor, Niels Stensen, was one of the first people to study fossils carefully. When he was shown a tongue stone, a fossil then believed by most people to grow naturally in the wild, he pointed out that it looked very much like a shark's tooth. A century later, British engineer William Smith (1769–1839) realized that different layers of rock contained different kinds of fossils. He formed the theory that

The fossilized tooth of an early shark

Above These fossils are the remains of sea creatures that lived 30 million years ago.

Below William Smith.

Fossils and fakes

In the eighteenth century, Johannes Beringer was one of Germany's most respected physicians. He was also interested in antiquities and fossils. One day, three students led Dr. Beringer to some very unusual fossils that included a scorpion-like creature, a spider spinning a web, and a bird sucking nectar from a fragile flower. They even found the fossilized remains of a clay tablet bearing Hebrew letters.

Dr. Beringer wrote a book about these finds that was published in 1726. Then he found an extraordinary fossil—a tablet bearing his own name. He was furious, and realized that the whole discovery had been a practical joke by the three jealous students to discredit his reputation.

rocks with the same fossils were formed at the same time. He also realized that the deeper the layer, the older it was.

Lamarck and Cuvier

At the same time, Jean Baptiste Lamarck, a French naturalist, announced that fossils were the remains of living creatures that had evolved into better ones. His friend, Baron Georges Cuvier, an anatomist and palaeontologist, noticed families of animals shared characteristics. He pointed out that only members of the cat family had retractable claws, and that all animals with hooves were vegetarians. Cuvier realized that fossils

Below The colors of these mountains show the different layers, or strata, of the rocks. Each layer was formed more recently than the one below it.

Georges Cuvier (1769–1832) as a young man

13

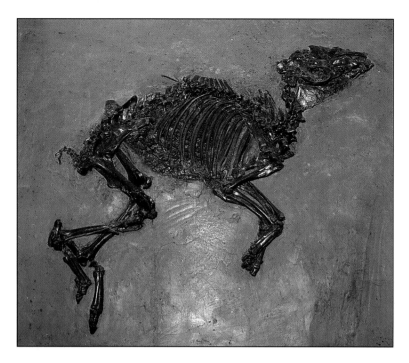

This fossil of a horse is about 55 million years old. It looks much like the skeleton of a modern horse but is different enough to show that it belonged to a creature that died out long ago.

must have come from extinct animals, because they are structurally different from similar living creatures. He decided that worldwide floods must occasionally have wiped out entire species of animals, and God had then created new ones to take their place. Later, he adapted his idea to accept the fact that some animals could have died out and not been replaced. But he would never agree that humans had also evolved. "No one will ever find a human fossil," he declared. He was to be proved wrong.

The 45,000 dollar man

In 1868, George Hull, a cigar maker from Binghamton, New York, fooled thousands of people with a fake human fossil. He commissioned a Chicago mason to carve a gigantic man out of limestone. Then his cousin buried the statue on his farm near Cardiff, New York.

A year later, Hull pretended to find it while digging a well. Thousands of people flocked to see the giant fossil, for which they were charged one dollar.

By the time their deception was discovered by newspaper reporters, Hull and his cousin had made nearly $45,000.

FOSSILS UNDER THE SEA

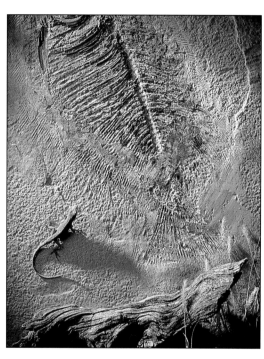

THERE are many more fossils of water-dwelling creatures than of the plants and animals that lived on land. This is because living creatures appeared in the water billions of years before they did on land. Also, water dwellers were often buried in silt, mud, or sand before their bodies could rot away, and many of them had hard shells and bones that fossilized well. The corpses of land dwellers often fell on hard ground, where they were eaten by other animals or destroyed by the elements. Thousands of extinct plants that grew far from water probably perished without leaving a record of their existence.

The fossil of a jellyfish from the Ediacara Hills in Australia. Fossils found in these hills date back to the Precambrian period.

A modern salamander face-to-face with the fossil of a prehistoric fish

The age of fishes
The first sea creatures appeared about 3.5 billion years ago. They were cytoids, or one-celled organisms, whose fossils have survived to this day.

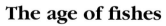

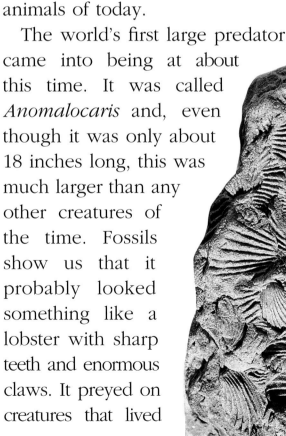

Anomalocaris might have looked like this. It had a circular mouth with sharp teeth on its underside.

About 2.5 billion years later, multicelled creatures came into being and slowly evolved into the first animals. Some of them resembled slugs, while others looked like blobs of jelly clinging to the seabed.

Then around 570 million years ago, in the Cambrian period, there was an explosion of aquatic activity. Helped along by increased amounts of oxygen in the water, the underwater life forms evolved into the ancestors of the fish and animals of today.

The world's first large predator came into being at about this time. It was called *Anomalocaris* and, even though it was only about 18 inches long, this was much larger than any other creatures of the time. Fossils show us that it probably looked something like a lobster with sharp teeth and enormous claws. It preyed on creatures that lived

Brachiopod fossils from the Silurian period. Their shells have left a distinct pattern in the rock.

on the seabed. Such new predators forced other creatures to evolve defense mechanisms. The *Wixwaxia,* a round creature that looked like a small turtleshell, sprouted scales, and the brachiopods developed hard shells. Maybe some of the creatures failed to defend themselves properly and maybe this is why they became extinct, leaving only fossils to show that they ever existed. Others, such as the brachiopods, survive to this day.

Trilobites

The most common sea creature in Cambrian times was the trilobite. This was an oval creature, varying from half an inch to thirty inches long. It had a hard shell that it shed as it grew. Its body was divided into segments: Each segment had one pair of legs for walking and another pair for paddling. Trilobites became extinct at the end of the Permian period, about 250 million years ago, but many fossils have been found worldwide.

Below This model shows what a trilobite might have looked like.

Many sizes of trilobite fossils have been found. Trilobites lived in all of the prehistoric world's oceans, mostly on the seabed.

This painting shows how a coastal area might have looked in the Ordovician period, about 460 million years ago.

The Cambrian times were followed by the Ordovician period, which lasted from 510 to 438 million years ago and saw the development of the first creatures with backbones, called vertebrates. They were the ancestors of fish, and they looked much like the lampreys and hagfishes of today. From fossils found in North America, we know that they had tough scales around their heads and the front of their bodies. They had no limbs, but scaly paddles protruded from their heads. They had no jaws, either; they simply sucked their victims into their mouths.

In the next period, the Silurian, which lasted up to 410 million years ago, the first animals and plants appeared on land. Fossils of ferns and mosses have been discovered in northern Europe and North America.

Gristly fish

Meanwhile, in the sea, the first jawed fish appeared. They had skeletons made of gristle or cartilage; not bone. Their descendants are still around today in the form of sharks and rays.

Enter the sea scorpion

The first sea scorpions appeared in Silurian times. Called Eurypterids, they lived in both fresh- and seawater. They were aggressive hunters and they terrorized small creatures, which they could sting with their flailing tails.

During the Devonian period, they evolved into ferocious monsters, some of which were over 10 feet long. They were the ancestors of the scorpions, the first land animals.

Some of today's scorpions are just as aggressive as their sea-dwelling ancestors. They have a long body ending in a poisonous sting, which can sometimes be deadly to humans. The largest scorpion of all, the tropical emperor, can grow up to seven inches long.

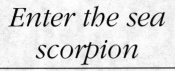

This fossil of a Devonian sea scorpion, or *Eurypterid*, has been preserved in fine siltstone.

Modern scorpions have eight legs and two extra front "legs" with pincers used for grabbing prey. The outer casing of a scorpion is thick, tough, and almost totally waterproof.

Swamp-dweller

Dipterus *was a type of lungfish that lived in the late Devonian period. Toward the end of the Devonian, Earth's climate became warmer. The planet suffered periods of torrential rain followed by intense droughts.*

A model of the lungfish *Dipterus*

Some seas shrank to become warm, shallow swamps, in which the water contained little oxygen. Lungfish adapted to living in these conditions. They developed lungs and took in oxygen by swimming to the surface of the swamp and gulping in air.

Fish with
bony skeletons
also appeared around
this time in warm lagoons around the planet.

In the next period, the Devonian, which started 410 million years ago, bony fish multiplied and gradually developed into two types. The first type —ray-finned fish—later developed into the bony fish of today. The second type—fleshy-finned fish —included lungfish, which had lungs and could breathe air as well as water, and coelacanths. Both of these can still be found today.

This South American lungfish has lungs on either side of the throat. If the river or lake it lives in dries up, it can survive for a long time by breathing air.

By the Carboniferous age, which began 355 million years ago, every known class of fish and sea creature had been formed. On dry land, the pace of evolution quickened. Scorpions, winged insects, and the *Tetrapod*, an amphibian with four legs, appeared.

Early amphibians, such as these *Ichthyostega*, developed from fish. The fish's fins gradually became legs.

A fossilized fish found in the limestone quarries of Bolca

Bolca—the sea of fossils

Outside the little village of Bolca, close to the Italian city of Verona, is a series of limestone quarries and hills riddled with passages and tunnels. Fossils excavated from various sites there include mackerel, sea pike, seaweed, giant sea urchins, rays, palm trees, worms, tortoises, feathers, jellyfish, sharks' teeth, and a 6.5-foot-long crocodile. They range from extinct prehistoric species to relatively modern animals that are found in tropical climates, proving that Bolca was once a tropical lagoon. Unlike fossils found in other places, many of the Bolca specimens have retained their color and other details, including skin and tissue.

FOSSILS OF LAND ANIMALS

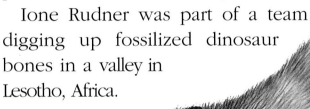

FOR years, people believed that mammals appeared on Earth around ninety million years ago, toward the end of the dinosaur age. But in 1966, the discovery of mammal bones and teeth in South Africa proved that mammals had been sharing the planet with dinosaurs long before that.

Ione Rudner was part of a team digging up fossilized dinosaur bones in a valley in Lesotho, Africa.

Megazostrodon. This tiny animal is believed to be the ancestor of the platypus. Both are egg-laying mammals.

One of the diggers found a fragment of bone that did not seem to belong to a dinosaur, and threw it away. But Rudner picked it up and studied it carefully. She thought that it looked similar to the jawbone of a mammal. Rudner unearthed more bones, and then spent several months rebuilding the skeleton. When it was finished, it was the size of a small shrew. It was a small mammal and was given the name *Megazostrodon.* It had lived 200 million years ago, near the beginning of the dinosaur age.

A mammoth on display in St. Petersburg, Russia. It was excavated from the ice in Siberia in the nineteenth century.

The mighty mammoth

Many of the mammals that lived on our planet in prehistoric times are now extinct, and we only know that they existed because of their fossils. Most of them were quite small compared with the largest modern mammals. Among the large mammals was the mammoth, a huge, elephant-like animal whose hairy shoulders stood 13 feet above the ground.

Mammoths first appeared around 1.6 million years ago, during the Pleistocene epoch.

The woolly mammoth lived in Europe and Siberia during the last Ice Age, which ended about 10,000 years ago. It fed on plants growing in the tundra.

They lived in Africa, Europe, Asia, and North America, and spent all their time looking for food to satisfy their enormous appetites. The smaller woolly mammoth inhabited the frozen ground regions around the Arctic, the region known as permafrost. Its thick wool protected it from the merciless weather. In Siberia, Russia, the bodies of thousands of woolly mammoths were preserved deep frozen in the intense cold of the permafrost.

Above This comb with carvings of a lion, unicorn, and eagle was made from mammoth ivory.

The ivory trade

About two thousand years ago, people in Mongolia discovered the mammoths' precious remains. They cut off the enormous tusks and sold them to merchants. The tusks were then carved into sword handles, boxes, souvenirs, and cooking pots. Mammoth ivory became an international business, but the ivory hunters had no idea they were digging up precious fossils. Some people thought that the bones and tusks belonged to giant underground rats.

Others believed that they were the remains of evil giants that were left out of Noah's ark during the biblical flood.

This skeleton belonged to a species of mammoth called *Mammuthus columbi.* When alive, the creature was 13 feet high and resembled a giant elephant. It lived in the warmer parts of North America more than 10,000 years ago before becoming extinct. This mammoth was a later relative of the woolly mammoth.

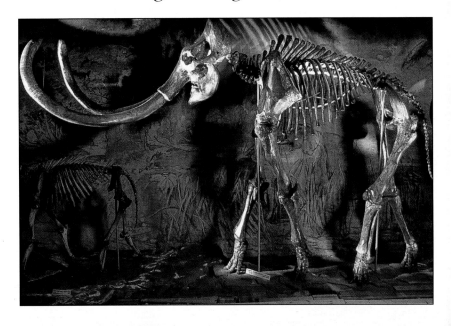

The mastodon's last supper

Some fossils can show us what extinct animals and early people used to eat. Experts believed that the mastodon, a type of mammoth, used to devour the branches of tough trees such as the spruce. But in 1989, some builders found a heap of mastodon bones in a bog in Ohio. Experts found traces of water lilies and pondweed in its stomach. There were also bacteria in the animals's intestines, too, which the experts brought back to life after nearly 12,000 years.

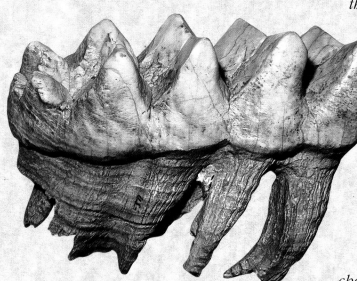

The study of the mastodon's remains also revealed that the animal had been killed and butchered by human beings. They had chopped up its carcass and hidden the flesh and bones at the bottom of a lake. For some reason, they never came back for the meat. The lake had gradually turned into a bog, sealing the mastodon's remains.

Above A fossil tooth of a mastodon from the late Pleistocene epoch

Tales of the strange animals from the permafrost attracted the attention of explorers and zoologists. In 1692, a Dutch zoologist, Evert Ysbrandt Ides, visited China. He guessed rightly that the skeletons belonged to a prehistoric relative of the elephant. A Siberian explorer, Michael Wolochowiz, reported seeing a rotting mammoth carcass being savaged by wolves on the banks of a river. His report astounded and alarmed all of Russia. Could these creatures still be roaming the tundra?

The body in the ice

In 1799, a hunter named Shumakov found a whole mammoth trapped in a gigantic block of ice near the Lena River. Two years later, he returned and found that all the ice had melted and the mammoth was exposed. He told his friend Roman Boltunov, an ivory dealer, about his discovery.

Early people hunting woolly mammoths about 35,000 years ago. Rhinoceroses were also alive at the time, and they ate the same vegetation as the mammoths.

Boltunov made detailed sketches of the creature and sent them to Professor M. I. Adams at the Academy of Sciences in St. Petersburg. The professor traveled to the Lena River. By the time he got there, wolves had eaten almost all of one side of the mammoth, but the other side was still intact. Adams's men shipped the creature back to St. Petersburg. This unusual kind of fossil was deep-frozen, with the unrotted flesh still intact on the skeleton.

At last the riddle of the tusks had been solved. Everyone could see that they belonged to an extinct creature—the woolly mammoth.

The massive skull of West Runton mammoth being excavated. Its long, curved tusks are still attached in their sockets.

A mammoth in the cliffs

One day in the autumn of 1990, amateur naturalists Harold and Margaret Hems were walking along the beach at West Runton in Norfolk, England, when they saw something sticking out from the cliff face. On closer examination, it turned out to be a very large animal bone. It was the beginning of a great find: A huge skeleton was hidden in the cliffs.

The bones belonged to a large ancestor of the woolly mammoth, known as Mammuthus trogontherii, *which lived about 600,000 years ago. The animal had been in its prime when it died at about 40 years old. It would have stood 13 feet high at the shoulder and weighed 10 tons—twice as heavy as a modern African elephant. Each of its tusks was curved and measured more than 10 feet long. Its feet were missing—they had probably been eaten by hyenas soon after the mammoth died. We know that hyenas roamed England until only about 20,000 years ago, along with bears, rhinoceroses, and bison.*

The site of the excavation at the base of the cliff

Above A prehistoric coastal scene, showing an ichthyosaur (**rear**), a plesiosaur (**front**), and a teleosaur (**right**)

Reptiles rule

Today, there are only four types of reptile: lizards and snakes; turtles and tortoises; crocodiles and alligators; and tuataras—strange lizards that live only in New Zealand. But fossils have shown us that, in Mesozoic times, there were many more. The different species included dinosaurs and crocodiles, which lived on the land, ichthyosaurs and plesiosaurs, which lived in the sea, and the flying pterosaurs, which looked like giant bats with sharp, toothed beaks.

In 1810, an 11-year-old schoolgirl named Mary Anning discovered the first skeleton of an ichthyosaur, near Lyme Regis, England. At first, she thought it was the remains of a crocodile. Mary went on to discover many more fossils and is now regarded as one of the pioneers of fossil hunting.

Mary Anning (1799–1847). In addition to the ichthyosaur, she also discovered the first plesiosaurs and, in 1828, the first pterosaur fossils.

Powerful and deadly

Perhaps the deadliest animal was the saber-toothed cat, or *Smilodon*. It was about the same size as the modern lion, but it had enormous teeth like daggers. It also had much more powerful claws than those of modern big cats.

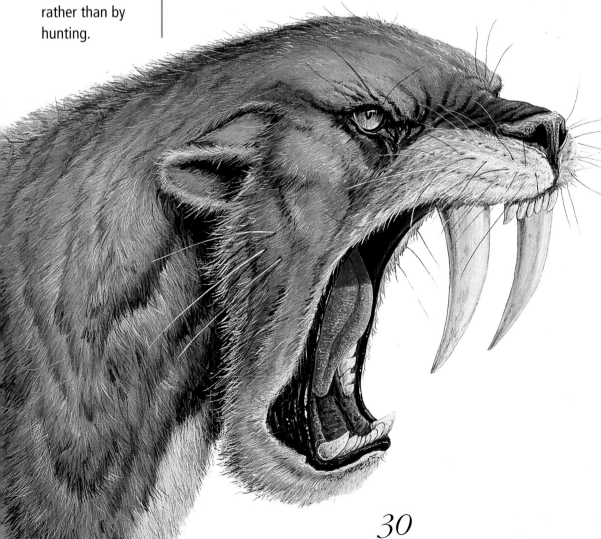

Below The many fossils at Rancho La Brea showed that saber-toothed cats had weak back legs. Because of this, some palaeontologists believe they fed by preying on weak, young, and dying animals rather than by hunting.

In 1906, the first fossilized remains of saber-toothed cats in the world were uncovered at Rancho La Brea, in what is now Los Angeles, CA. Their teeth were 10 inches long and curved like knives. About seven hundred skulls were found. Experts also found the fossilized remains of an extinct vulture. Its claws were wrapped around the skeleton of a drowned Native American.

Above A mammoth trapped in the oily pools of Rancho La Brea was easy prey for hungry predators such as saber-toothed cats, wolves, and huge teratorn vultures. At Rancho La Brea, underground oil oozed up into swamps. During the last Ice Age, it was covered by water, making it a deadly trap.

THE QUEST FOR HUMAN FOSSILS

THE bones and fossils of dead people have helped scientists to put together the story of human evolution from *Australopithecus afarensis*, the earliest humanlike creature, or hominid, right up to *Homo sapiens* (the scientific name for modern humans). For hundreds and thousands of years, the mystery was answered only by superstition and religious beliefs. It is only recently that we have come to accept that humans are descended from the same species that produced apes and monkeys.

The first hominids

Charles Darwin (1809–82), a British naturalist, established the idea of evolution. This theory suggested that all living things, including humans, originated from the same primitive life forms of millions of years ago. He guessed that humans had emerged in Africa long before they were believed to have appeared in Asia, about one million years ago.

Left Fossil hand bones of *Australopithecus afarensis*, the oldest hominid ancestor of modern humans

Below A modern human hand

Left Charles Darwin

31

His statements found favor with many scholars all over the world. They also made him a lot of enemies, especially among devout Christians, who believed that God had created humans.

In search of our origins

Inspired by Darwin's ideas, scientists started looking for human fossils in Africa. In 1932, a palaeoanthropologist named Louis Leakey discovered the remains of a creature called *Proconsul*, which was an ancestor of the earliest apes and monkeys. Leakey and his wife, Mary, later found the remains of some human ancestors.

Above This cartoon from 1874 shows Charles Darwin with one of his "ancestors."

Below Stages in the development of humans: *Australopithecus afarensis* (**1**), *Homo habilis* (**2**), *Homo erectus* (**3**), *Homo neanderthalensis* (**4**), and *Homo sapiens* (**5**)

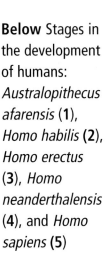

These included fossil bones belonging to *Homo habilis,* which dated from about two million years ago, and *Homo erectus,* which lived between about 1.6 million years ago and 250,000 years ago. Most scientists now believe that modern humans —*Homo sapiens*—first began to develop from *Homo erectus* about a million years ago.

Lucy

Other important discoveries that have been made around the world, including skulls and even complete skeletons, have helped scientists chart the course of human evolution.

One notable find was that of the skeleton of an *Australopithecus afarensis* female, nicknamed Lucy, which was discovered by Donald Johanson in 1974. It was believed to be the oldest remains ever found of an upright hominid.

The skeleton of Lucy

The 230-foot-long trail of hominid footprints found by Mary Leakey. The prints were made by two adults and possibly a child walking in the adults' footsteps. The prints on the far left of the picture were left by a *Hipparion*, an extinct three-toed horse.

Lucy lived between four million and three million years ago, and her discovery in Ethiopia established the fact that hominids had begun to walk upright long before they developed the bigger brain that is normally associated with *Homo erectus* and *Homo sapiens*.

In 1976, Mary Leakey discovered the fossils of the oldest hominid footprints in the world, in Laetoli, Tanzania. They had been left at the base of a volcano about 3.75 million years ago. A group of hominids had walked over a layer of damp, gray ash that had been released by the active volcano, and then the sun had come out, hardening the ash and preserving their footprints forever. The find proved that some primates had started to walk on two feet at least 3.75 million years ago. Then, in 1991 in Ethiopia, John Fleagle and Solomon Yirga discovered seven teeth belonging to the same species as Lucy— *Australopithecus afarensis*.

Below Fossil jaw bones and teeth of *Australopithecus afarensis.* They were found in the Afar region of Ethiopia between 1973 and 1977.

They are believed to be nearly 4.5 million years old, and are the earliest hominid remains ever found.

A Pazyryk burial

On a spring day 2,400 years ago, a lavish funeral took place at Ukok in the Altai Mountains of southern Siberia, Russia. A 25-year-old woman, dressed in fine clothes, was lowered into an enormous grave lined with logs. She was placed in a coffin and her head turned to the east according to the custom of the Pazyryks, an ancient tribe of seminomadic people. Plates of mutton and horse meat were set next to the coffin, along with a bronze knife and other implements. A beautiful vase was filled with drink and placed next to the food.

Left A skull of *Australopithecus africanus*, which lived between three million and 2.5 million years ago. These hominids were taller than *Australopithecus afarensis* and had a larger brain.

The site of the Pazyryk burial

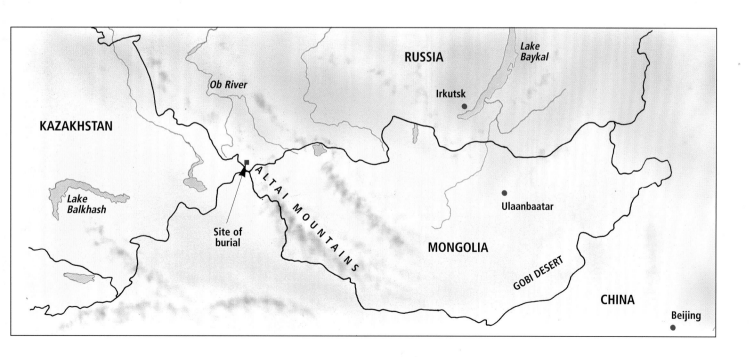

The men killed six horses with their sharp axes and lowered their bodies into the tomb. The woman's relatives and friends ate a meal in her honor, then the tomb was sealed and a tall burial mound, or kurgan, was built upon it.

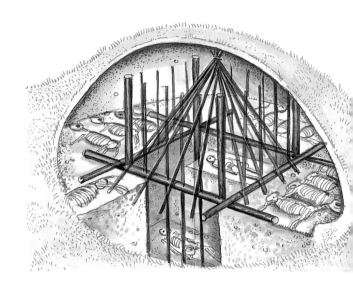

After the ceremony, the mourners left the area in search of other grazing grounds for their flocks. Soon it started to rain and water filled the tomb. That winter, the water froze, preserving the woman's body, the horses, and all the objects. The Pazyryk people passed into history, and their story and culture were forgotten almost completely.

Digging through history

In 1993, the tomb was discovered by a Russian archaeologist named Natalya Poslosmak. Scholars were eager to find out as much as they could about the vanished Pazyryk culture, but most of the graves they had discovered had been looted and destroyed.

Above This illustration shows the burial of a Steppe nomad chieftain. The Steppes extend from the far east to the far west of Russia. The chieftain was buried at the bottom of a pit, and his servants were buried at a shallower level, with weapons and horses.

The well-preserved body of the young Pazyryk woman found buried in the ice

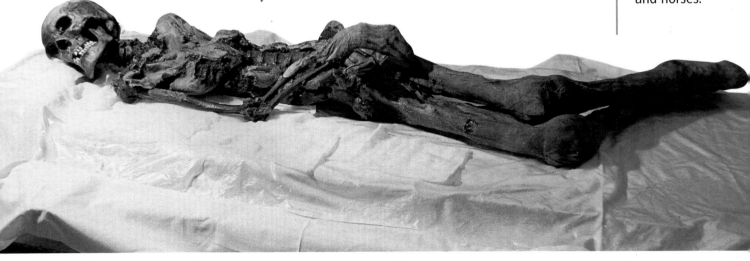

36

The mummy's curse

The ancient Egyptians perfected the art of preserving dead bodies by mummifying them. They believed that the soul could survive only if the body remained intact.

Early attempts to make mummies failed, and the bodies rotted away, but later attempts were very successful.

Mummification involved removing the brain, which was thrown away, and the inner organs, which were put in special jars. The heart was left in the body, which was soaked in a preserving fluid called natron. The body was then dried and stuffed with rags and wrapped in bandages.

Strange stories about the magical powers of ancient mummies were very popular. An Egyptian princess who had disobeyed her powerful father, Pharaoh Akhenaten, was murdered. To prevent the girl's spirit from traveling to the afterlife, the killers chopped off her right hand and buried it separately. In 1890, a mummified hand was given to Lord Louis Hamon and his wife by an Egyptian sheik.

Lord and Lady Hamon, having tried unsuccessfully to get rid of the mummy's hand, locked it in a safe. Thirty years later, terrified at noticing new flesh growing on the old bones, they put the hand on the fire. There was a clap of thunder as it caught fire. The door burst open and the princess's ghost glided into the room. She rescued her hand from the flames and disappeared. Whatever the truth of the story, Lord and Lady Hamon had to be treated for shock in a London hospital.

Above A mummy being X-rayed. The skull can be seen on the X-ray films on the right.

Below Two canopic jars used for storing the internal organs of a mummy. The baboon-headed jar (**left**) was for the lungs, and the human-headed jar for the liver.

The body of an Egyptian mummy. The bandages were removed in 1834.

In 1990, Poslosmak traveled to Ukok with five students. They found lots of kurgans on the steppes. The first one they examined contained the skeletons of two warriors and ten horses, along with knives, axes, and other weapons. On top of it was a second burial dating from the seventh century B.C. but it was not a Pazyryk, but a member of an unknown nomadic tribe.

In 1993, Poslosmak and her assistants began digging in a large kurgan next to the Russian border. After removing all the stones above the tomb, Poslosmak saw a big hole: Grave robbers must have broken in. The team kept digging and soon unearthed a man's corpse inside a rotting coffin and three dead horses. Poslosmak's heart missed a beat. Here was yet another example of an unknown people burying their dead on top of a Pazyryk grave. Perhaps the looters had only got this far too.

The team continued digging with renewed effort. The tomb underneath seemed to be frozen and untouched.

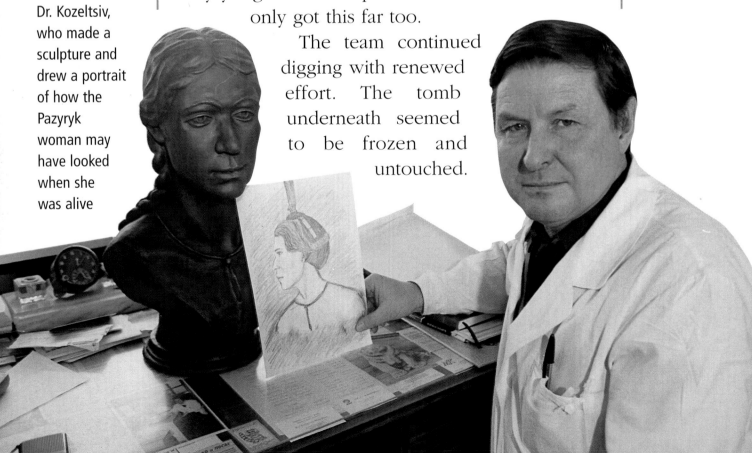

Dr. Kozeltsiv, who made a sculpture and drew a portrait of how the Pazyryk woman may have looked when she was alive

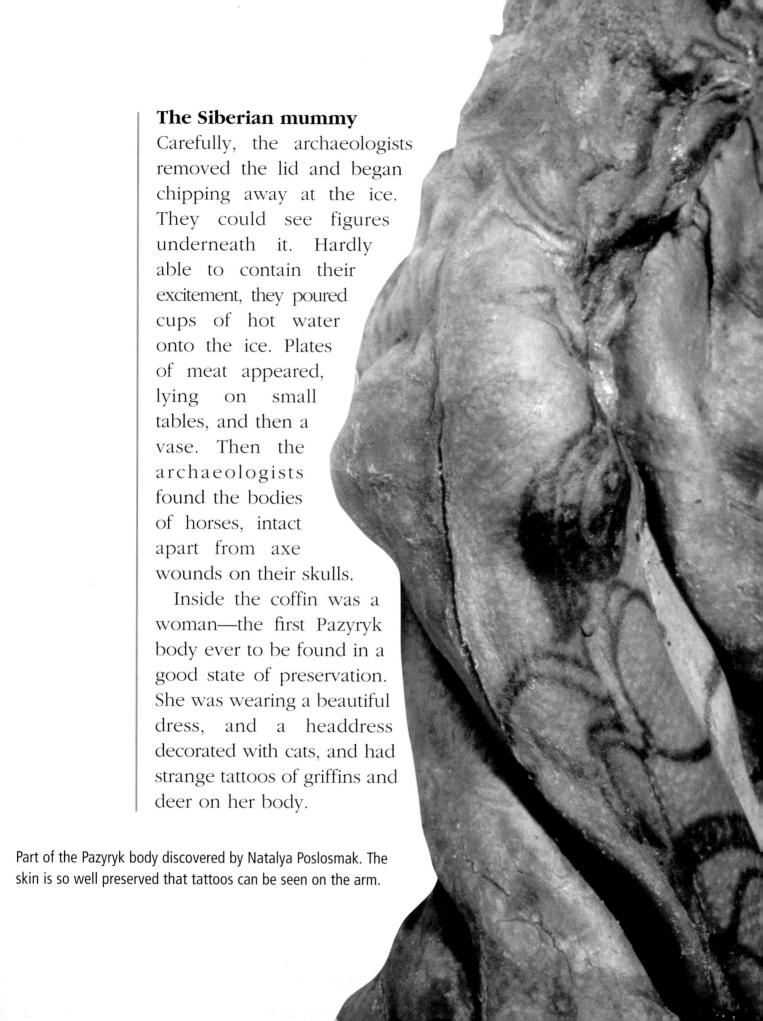

The Siberian mummy

Carefully, the archaeologists removed the lid and began chipping away at the ice. They could see figures underneath it. Hardly able to contain their excitement, they poured cups of hot water onto the ice. Plates of meat appeared, lying on small tables, and then a vase. Then the archaeologists found the bodies of horses, intact apart from axe wounds on their skulls.

Inside the coffin was a woman—the first Pazyryk body ever to be found in a good state of preservation. She was wearing a beautiful dress, and a headdress decorated with cats, and had strange tattoos of griffins and deer on her body.

Part of the Pazyryk body discovered by Natalya Poslosmak. The skin is so well preserved that tattoos can be seen on the arm.

THE WORLD OF LIVING FOSSILS

SINCE life first began on our planet, about 3.5 billion years ago, living organisms have developed and evolved to produce the enormous variety of plants, animals, and other life forms we know today. Many millions of creatures have died out completely—dinosaurs, for example—or have developed into other animals. But some others seem to have stopped evolving long ago. Scientists have found fossils of creatures that are almost identical to animals living today. These creatures that have stayed almost unchanged for millions of years are sometimes called living fossils.

The fossil of a cockroach

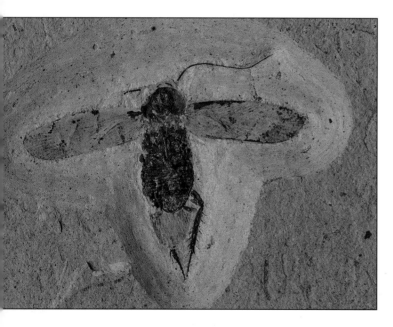

The indestructible cockroach

The cockroach is one of the oldest insects in the world. It first appeared on the planet about 320 million years ago. One cockroach fossil that was found in North America dates back three hundred million years. It shows the creature very much like it is today, with huge, waxy wings and long legs.

Tracking the okapi

Sir Harry H. Johnston from Great Britain was determined to find the okapi, an animal that was believed to have been extinct for thirty million years. Fossils of the creature existed, and they showed it had a head like a giraffe's, hooves like those of a goat, and striped back legs similar to a zebra's.

The explorer and writer Sir Harry Hamilton Johnston (1858–1927)

When Johnston read that Congo tribespeople in Africa had reported seeing such a beast, he set out to find it. Most people laughed, but Sir Harry would not give up. He searched the jungle until, in 1906, he found and captured a living okapi. It had a 20-inch tongue that it used to clean its own eyes.

Below The okapi Johnston was looking for. The species is now called *Okapia johnstoni*.

The modern cockroach is almost impossible to kill. It can go for three months without food and at least one month without water. It has been known to survive by eating paper, soap, rope, and shoelaces. Special suckers on the cockroach's feelers allow it to detect poison in food before it eats it. Sensors in its knees allow it to detect the slightest motion, making it almost impossible to catch.

A female American cockroach with a recently formed egg capsule at the end of her body. Like all insects, cockroaches have a basic body structure—a skeleton on the outside and a body in three parts: a head with two antennae, the thorax with three pairs of legs, and the abdomen for food digestion and reproductive organs.

Cockroaches have infiltrated every corner of the earth except the Arctic and Antarctic. They move mostly by night, often traveling by hiding in cars, buses, and other forms of transportation used by humans. Everywhere they go, they carry dangerous germs.

All of the four thousand types of cockroaches breed incredibly quickly. One pair can generate 400,000 offspring. The Surinam cockroach does not even need a male to produce young. It simply creates exact copies, or clones, of itself. Worst of all, the cockroach can make itself immune to pesticides encountered by its ancestors. No wonder it hasn't needed to evolve for millions of years.

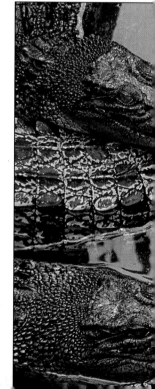

Crocodiles

The crocodile first appeared at the end of the Triassic period, about 205 million years ago. It was a direct descendant of thecodonts, earlier reptiles that lived mostly in the water. The first crocodiles lived entirely on the land, although their descendants have returned to life in the water.

Today's crocodiles behave very much like their ancestors. They spend most of their time lurking in shallow waters and venturing onto dry land in search of victims. The most dangerous are the saltwater and the Nile crocodiles. They are man-eaters and have been known to terrorize entire communities.

At the end of the line

Another creature that seems to have stopped evolving is the coelacanth. This curious fish has remained unchanged since the Devonian period, some 410 to 355 million years ago. The first coelacanth fossils were found in 1839, and people believed they had become extinct in the Cretaceous period, 135 to 65 million years ago. More fossils turned up, and eventually 80 specimens of coelacanth had been identified.

Then in 1938, a fisherman caught a coelacanth off the South African coast.

Unfortunately, the fish did not survive. The fisherman handed it to the curator of a local museum, and the curator passed it on to a fossil expert who identified it as a coelacanth. He offered a reward to anyone who could catch a live coelacanth. In 1952, someone succeeded in doing this. Since then, more have been caught and some have even been filmed swimming near Madagascar.

No one knows how many other animals that are thought to be extinct are hiding in the remote parts of our planet, waiting to be discovered.

A living coelacanth photographed off the Comoros Islands between Madagascar and the African mainland

TIME LINE

1692

Evert Ysbrandt Ides identifies skeletons found in China as belonging to prehistoric relative of elephant

1769

Birth of William Smith, who identified strata in rocks

1799

Shumakov finds whole mammoth in ice near Lena River, Russia

1809

Birth of Charles Darwin, who first put forward the idea that humans and apes evolved from the same ancestors

1810

Mary Anning finds first fossilized ichthyosaur

1839

Sir Richard Owen identifies bone belonging to extinct bird, the moa. First coelacanth fossils found

1849

Owen assembles entire moa skeleton

1906

Fossils of saber-toothed cats found at Rancho La Brea. Sir Harry Johnston finds living okapi in Africa

1932

Louis Leakey discovers remains of *Proconsul*

1938

First coelacanth found in sea

1952

First live coelacanth caught

1966

Bones and teeth of 200-million-year-old mammal, *Megazostrodon*, found in Lesotho, Africa, by Ione Rudner

1974

Donald Johanson finds Lucy, an *Australopithecus afarensis* skeleton

1976

Mary Leakey finds oldest fossilized hominid footprints

1978

Michael Voorhies finds large number of fossilized creatures in Nebraska

1993

Natalya Poslosmak excavates ancient Pazyryk tomb in Russia

46

GLOSSARY

Abdomen The middle part of an animal's body.

Amphibian A creature that can breathe in and out of water.

Anthropologist A person who studies the origins of humans as well as his beliefs, characteristics, and social behavior.

Cataracts A disease that clouds the eye.

Griffin A legendary creature with wings, the body of a lion, and an eagle's head.

Hominid A member of the human family, including modern humans and our extinct ancestors.

Organism Any living thing, including bacteria.

Palaeontologist Someone who studies fossils to determine the story of the world's evolution.

Prehistoric From the time before the written word.

Resin The sticky sap produced by some trees.

Siberian Someone or something that comes from Siberia, a cold, vast region in Russia.

Tundra The vast, frozen region in the north of the planet.

Vertebrate A creature with a spine.

Zoologist A scientist who studies animals.

FURTHER INFORMATION

BOOKS

Cork, Barbara and Struan Reid. *Archaeology.* Tulsa, OK: EDC Press, 1985.

McIntosh, Jane. *Archeology.* Eyewitness Books. New York: Alfred A. Knopf, 1994.

Place, Robin. *Bodies from the Past.* Digging Up the Past. New York: Thomson Learning, 1996.

Nardo, Don. *Dinosaurs.* Exploring the Unknown. San Diego: Lucent Books, 1994.

Sabin, Louis. *Fossils.* Mahwah, NJ: Troll Associates, 1985.

Walker, Cyril and David J. Ward. *Fossils.* Eyewitness Handbooks. New York: Dorling Kindersley, 1992.

Pope, Joyce and Stella Stilwell. *Living Fossils.* Austin, TX: Raintree Steck-Vaughn, 1992.

Gamlin, Linda. *Origins of Life.* Today's World. New York: Fanklin Watts, 1988.

Guilaine, Jen. *Prehistory.* New York: Facts on File, 1991.

INDEX